Susan Herbert

MOVIE CATS

With 57 illustrations

Thames & Hudson

The Sirens

'See what the cats in the back room will have.'

Moggy Dearest

Glamour Puss

Sex Kitten

'Is that a mouse in your pocket, or are you just glad to see me?'

The
Comedians

'Another fishy mess you've gotten me into.'

The Manx Brothers

Charlie Catlin

The
Musicals

Dancing paw to paw

Top Cat

King of the Siamese

Soggy moggy

Wonderful Whiskers of Oz

The Sound of the Mouse-Trapp Family

'Diamond flea collars are a cat's best friend.'

'Everything Feline in America'

My Fur Lady

'I could have pranced all night....'

Historic Spectacles

'Thou shalt not covet thy neighbour's mouse.'

Cleocatra

Ben Purr

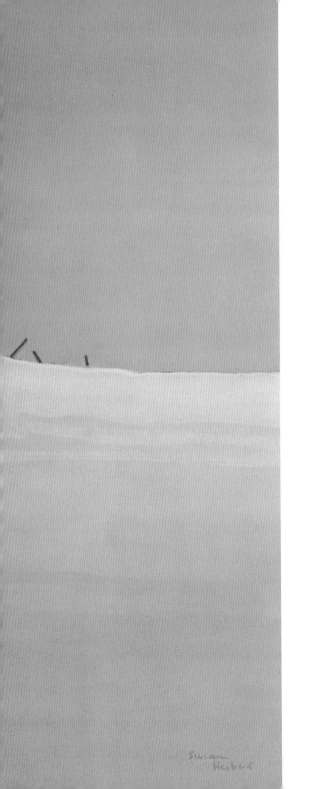

Paw Prints of Arabia

The Catiator

Drama & Romance

Susan Herbert

'Actually, I wouldn't mind sleeping with the fishes.'

Feline Kane

Russian Blues

Cat-nipped at the waist

'Meet me at the catflap, ma cherie.'

At the dance with Scarlett O'Hairball

The Red Mews

Rebel with Four Paws

A Brief Tail of Love

From Fur to Eternity

Cats-a-Blanca

'I know it's not a cat thing, but we may have to swim for it.'

The Good, the Bad, and the Tabby

Sam Spayed

Pussies Galore

'I'm ready for my close-up, Mr de Mew.'

Sourpuss

An Alfred Hitchcat masterpiece

Susan Herbert

Puss in Boots

Pussyfooting around

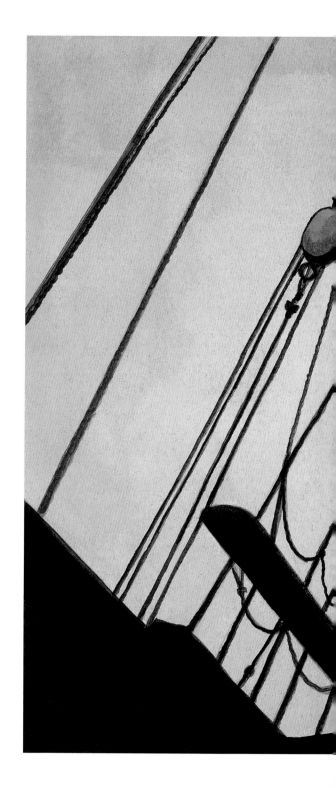

'Scaredy-Cat!'

The Cat of the Baskervilles

First published in 2006 in hardcover in the United States of America by
Thames & Hudson Inc., 500 Fifth Avenue, New York, New York 10110

thamesandhudsonusa.com

Library of Congress Catalog Card Number 2006900828

ISBN-13:   978-0-500-51308-8
ISBN-10:   0-500-51308-2

Printed and bound by Oriental Press, Dubai